IS, THINKS PEARL

PRAISE FOR *IS, THINKS PEARL*

'A character named Pearl, who like a pearl, is a perfect self-contained sphere of being. Who, like a pearl, is built from layer after layer of experience, rounding her into an acute observing eye. Who, like a pearl, has something gritty at her centre, something that enables her to play – with the inherent absurdity of the daily goings on in a town [...] Pearl is a power to disrupt the coatings of ordinariness, showing us its underneath: wildness, weirdness, tattiness... all of which she reforges as perhaps more habitable for herself and for the reader.'
Sophie Herxheimer, author of *Velkom to Inklandt*
(Short Books, 2017)

'Roll up, roll up, for this guided tour of a seaside town with the eponymous Pearl as your guide. Part mapping exercise, part biography, these poems will transport you to the apparently familiar land of the lido, library and liquor store before you even notice how the ordinary becomes surreal. [...] Watch out! This is poetry, where language is the most alchemical ingredient of all and there's a surprise around every corner. Alert to the smallest details of this world, alive to its simplest joys where 'even a pastry / the papers and two cigarettes is a kiss', Pearl will leave you at the end of your tour feeling well-travelled, well-fed and somewhat astonished.'
Jacqueline Saphra, author of *All My Mad Mothers*
(Nine Arches, 2017)

OTHER TITLES FROM THE EMMA PRESS

POETRY PAMPHLETS

how the first sparks became visible, by Simone Atangana Bekono,
tr. from Dutch by David Colmer
do not be lulled by the dainty starlike blossom, by Rachael Matthews
With others in your absence, by Zosia Kuczyńska
Sandsnarl, by Jon Stone
This House, by Rehema Njambi

SHORT STORIES

The Secret Box, by Daina Tabūna, tr. from Latvian by Jayde Will
Tiny Moons: A year of eating in Shanghai, by Nina Mingya Powles
Postcard Stories 2, by Jan Carson
Hailman, by Leanne Radojkovich

POETRY ANTHOLOGIES

Second Place Rosette: Poems about Britain
Everything That Can Happen: Poems about the Future
The Emma Press Anthology of Contemporary Gothic Verse
The Emma Press Anthology of Illness

BOOKS FOR CHILDREN

Poems the wind blew in, by Karmelo C Iribarren,
tr. from Spanish by Lawrence Schimel
My Sneezes Are Perfect, by Rakhshan Rizwan
The Bee Is Not Afraid of Me: A Book of Insect Poems
Cloud Soup, by Kate Wakeling

ART SQUARES

Menagerie, by Cheryl Pearson, illustrated by Amy Evans
One day at the Taiwan Land Bank Dinosaur Museum,
by Elīna Eihmane

is, thinks Pearl

Poems by Julia Bird

THE EMMA PRESS

First published in the UK in 2021 by The Emma Press Ltd.
Poems © Julia Bird 2021.

All rights reserved.

The right of Julia Bird to be identified as the author of this work has been asserted in accordance with the Copyright, Designs and Patents Act 1988.

ISBN 978-1-912915-87-3

A CIP catalogue record of this book
is available from the British Library.

Printed and bound in the UK
by the Holodeck, Birmingham.

The Emma Press
theemmapress.com
hello@theemmapress.com
Birmingham, UK

Supported using public funding by
ARTS COUNCIL ENGLAND
LOTTERY FUNDED

CONTENTS

Helium Pearl 1
Red Pearl 2
Clementine Pearl 3
Yellow-pink Pearl 5
Liquid Pearl 7
Plasticine Pearl 8
Buzz Pearl 10
Flash Pearl 11
Burnt Pearl 12
Oxblood Pearl 14
Brownstone Pearl 16
Fried Pearl 17
Tartare Pearl 18
Violette Pearl 20
Foaming Pearl 22
R.E.M. Pearl 24
Tactical Pearl 26

Acknowledgements 28
About the poet 29
About The Emma Press 30

Helium Pearl

The man who stands all day in the high street
selling helium balloons is, thinks Pearl,
weighed down by the cumulus of gas and foil
capping low above his head. The drag on him
of a hundred fat cartoons tugging their leads
like young dogs: what if he doesn't sell out,
what if his mate doesn't show when he said
he would – how could he herd this tangling,
bumbling stock to a sandwich or a coffee shop?
Pearl knows that even one small silver pup,
its two dimensions startled into three, will not
sit still in the changing room, sit still on the bus:
it only wants to drop and dive back to the sun.
Pearl thinks that, when the time comes, this
is what it might be like to mourn – to tie each
elevating death with a ribbon to your wrist
and feel its unexpected weight every time a door
revolves, or you're at the cinema in a front seat,
or you're putting on or you're taking off your coat.

Red Pearl

Pearl has never quite been on safari
though there was that one occasion
she was on the river-crossing route
for what must have been the hundredth time
when the bus stopped and the doors opened
and a pigeon toddled on. The terrier
already on board pricked an ear towards the bird
but his mind was mostly on the pet crate
on a small girl's lap – the twitch and scrabble
of a hamster with a heart like a fat red flea.
Buffalo. Elephant. Rhino, Leopard, Lion.
Pearl rang the bell and let the bus sail on
while she carried her shopping home.
A free-range chicken, outdoor-reared ham.

Clementine Pearl

The first time was a fluke.
Subsequently, Pearl made plans
to visit the Christmas shop
at the edge of town every
twenty-fifth of June; a day
when even if it isn't hot, it's light,
the day most likely the shop's
most empty of people wanting
winter or its antimatter
to take into their homes.
Not evergreen nor clementine,
not white fur nor silver star.
Pearl goes to the Christmas shop
in June like she goes to a museum –
to dote on artefacts and attitudes
from six months past; or she comes
as she would to a spa or some
centre of the law – for something to be
scrubbed off or struck through.
There are sharp-bright songs to be sung
in a temple to the future. She buys
a glass wren on a gold thread

or a spangled papier-mâché pear
or a string of bulbs with a slow flash
like a tame beast breathing and says
to the shopkeeper as she taps her card
Let it snow who says to her
as he wraps the gift *And also,*
let it snow.

Yellow-pink Pearl

Weekly, Pearl walks by
the marked-off section
of the brick back wall
of the leisure centre,
the one the council
sets aside for street art.
She likes the metal sugar
notes of the spray paint,
the orchestrated rattle-
hiss of two quiet boys
at once exhibiting
their bubble letter names,
and how the grass grows
in the crack between
the pavement and the wall
yellow-pink the one week
and silver-green the next.
Execution, repetition,
modulation thinks Pearl
when tasked with any type
of regular activity. Ten
dresses, ten different pairs
of gold daps is 100 looks.

Pre-each spring clean,
a word drawn in the dust
on the mantelpiece is an utterly
novel wish or curse.

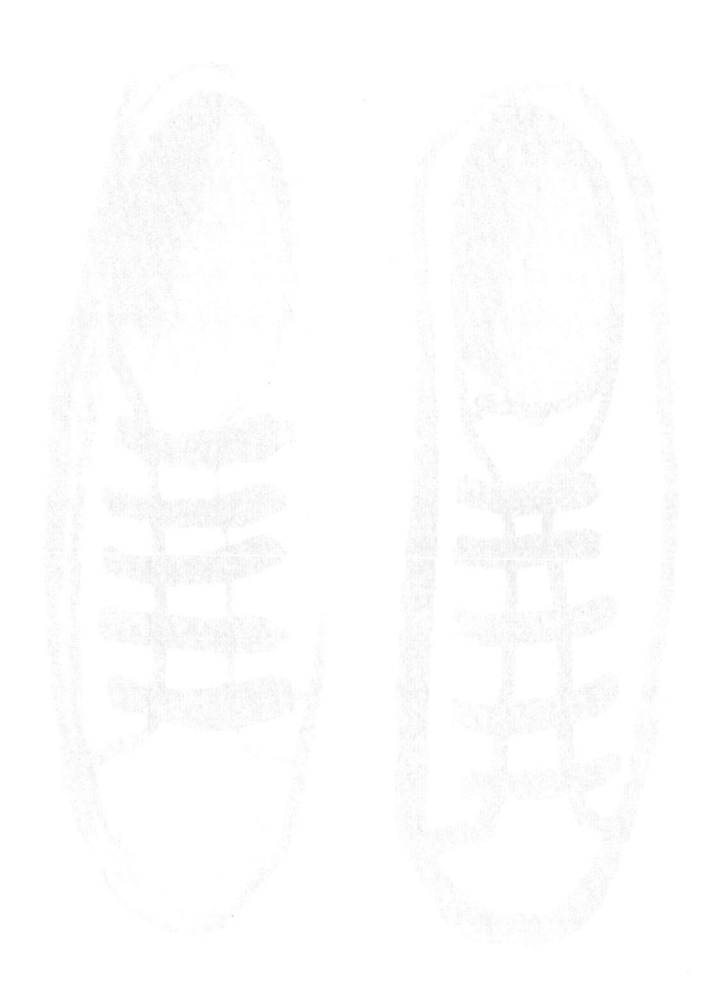

Liquid Pearl

When the Mayor reopens the lido
Pearl takes to the water
in a blow-up chair the shape
of a size fourteen flamingo,
a craft on which to drift along the filter current
from the shallow end to the deep
then scull the whole way back
with your non-bestseller hand
the length of an afternoon – though
if she ever does want to get out
there are people here eager
to sell her something sweet,
something cold or something salt.
From the tile pool edge,
the life-guard scans the liquid turquoise field,
the pink flamingo, Pearl's buttercup suit:
the three split tones of the sun.
Pearl drifts on. From her own breath
she has raised a throne.

Plasticine Pearl

It took a while for Pearl, at five,
to gather the difference between
a toy library and the toy shop,
but with her notable school skill
being the sorting of similar items –
wooden beads and building bricks –
into sets, she very soon picked up
that from the shop came the toys
that got played out: bottles of bubble
blown down to their rainbow dregs,
plasticine rolled into green worms
and red dogs then marbled
and marbled to grey, chemistry
kits whose squibs and crystals
flared or froze then turned silent
and inert. From the library
she borrowed a brown plastic till
with yellow buttons and a bell
and took turns to buy and sell herself
a multi-storey briefcase full
of cars to convoy or gridlock
or smash. Once she checked out
the same white bear for three fortnights

in a row. There were other children on the waiting list with terribly impatient dreams, but for those six weeks the name the bear responded to was Pearl's and Pearl's alone.

Buzz Pearl

In one of many idle moments, Pearl and her stylist
are leafing through the magazines. *Hair Weekly,
Hair Monthly, Quarterly Review of Hair. O the Beehive*
sighs the stylist, *the Man Bun and the Box Braids –
all these on the tip of my comb yet I must spend my days
flattening the excess of the ringleted or cooking curls
through the silk yards of the straight. And those –
you will have noticed – were just the simplest of the Bs.*
Mostly a salon's local climate is fine mist, cool blast.
Outdoors, a blood heat rain trickles down the necks
of the neighbouring shops: a baby goods emporium
and a Master Butchers whose door is propped open
by a jolly plaster apron-wearing pig. The stylist asks
if Pearl would like her water sparkling or still.
Grade One Buzz. Five Point Bob. Mermaid Balayage.

Flash Pearl

Sometimes, when taking books to or taking books
from Oxfam, Pearl will turn up a bookmark
tucked in a copy of *The Ghost Road* or *The God
Of Small Things*. As the confessional is
to the church, so the passport photo booth
is to the body of a shopping centre:
small room in a bigger one, curtains drawn
on the private moment, curtains drawn on
a narrative pivot. Halfway through
a paperback, here's a four-by-one of some girl
and her friend at the points the flash caught
the set-up, pay-off, beat and then the snort
of a joke saved up through the week then swapped
on a Saturday trip to town. Here's a stranger
and their flame, shine in their eyes and
kiss. Pearl recalls the booth stool on its screw
leg, the crank it took to make it pirouette.

Burnt Pearl

In a quiet café, over a glass of Sprite,
Pearl will tell you all about her plans
to buy up the ex-mattress factory,
gut it, convert it and open a Museum
of Light. She'll talk you up a blueprint,
then take you by the hand through
The Gallery of Bioluminescence where
beetles, plankton and decomposing wood
phase through their sequences and freckle
your dim and indoor face blue-green.
Perhaps you'd care to put your name
to a permanent display – The Illuminated
Sitting Room, where big red buttons
kindle in turn a cave-mouth campfire,
burnt gas in a glass orb, and four centuries
of crystal chandelier. Pearl says to stand
beneath their blizzard glints is to be
adored. Now walk towards the room where
screens show live feeds from every date-line:
where the moon skips off sky-scrapers
and seascapes, is never and always rising.
At closing time, Pearl would have you leave
with a bag of tea-lights and fireworks

and not discover till two weeks later
that the entrance ticket you tucked deep
in the back of your purse glows in the dark.

Oxblood Pearl

At almost six pm, the last toddler
has yet to leave the recreation ground
and the first teen has only just
arrived. Pearl keeps in mind
stories of the sandpit full of vodka
bottle glass, the inquisitive fingers
in the seesaw hinge. This hot day a boy
has sat down bump on the sponge
rubber base beneath the bucket swings,
poleaxed by the green shield bug which
landed on then took off from his arm:
the violation and the loss. And with one
slow oxblood-booted foot, a girl
sweeps herself round on the roundabout –
her hair dip-dyed the shade That Bitch
Lent Him Her Homework; her nails
picked down as far as polar bears
on paving slabs of ice. Age seven to ten,
from seven to nine pm, Pearl spent
Tuesdays learning how to knot a sling
or make a puppet from a gentleman's
white handkerchief. Here she stands now
at the top of the giant slide, the point

from which there are only two ways down:
the metal steps or the polished swoop.
The arc of the sun is a coin-toss, slowed.

Brownstone Pearl

Spring comes to the model village when the die-cast
ducklings are Blu-Tacked to the pocket mirror pond.
Autumn is a Co-op carrier full of russet
leaf crowns the model village manager installs
on one appointed day. Pearl feels for him
who can shrink all down to a one-in-twelve scale
except the special effects: his grocer grass cricket pitch
is slubbed with plate-sized daisies; a dusting of snow
buries the high-street balloon seller so just one
solid silver plastic puppy on a wire pokes out
from the drift. On a wet night, a foot-high snail
glides about the small municipal space, snotting up
the offices and sitting like a brownstone boulder
on the desk of the model village manager's model self.
Time was Pearl stole a villager – rocked her pegged feet
out of their position on the bowling green, snuck her
up her sleeve and took her home. There, she chipped off
her curls, filed down her skirt and redressed her in lace
and a real hair wig. Round her arms and shoulders,
Pearl painted blue and white convolvulus then found a spot
in the market square to re-root her. When the sun is out
the villager throws a shadow which is short and sharp
then nebulous and long, then short and sharp again.

Fried Pearl

Even the screen-light from a silenced phone
disturbs the other members of the rom-com crowd,
but before she powers down Pearl thumbs quickly through
a gallery of photos – twenty-four images of sweet
fried eggs, flump shrimps and blue jelly dolphins.
The name of this film is *Critics Are Always Divided.*

Tartare Pearl

Compiling her CV, Pearl recalls
the all-day seafood restaurant
she waitressed at for summer
after summer, and how she
knocked back oyster jokes
from diner after diner with *This
is nominative determinism and that
is lemon juice.* Two tropical aquaria,
two thousand gallons apiece, stood
top-lit and bubbling each side
of the door into the kitchen, full
of angels and puffers butting
their tight mouths against the glass.
Shoals of silver inches, each fish
red-lit or blue-lit with a central stroke,
zipped and skewed about the tank.
Pearl believed that when she turned
her back they grouped themselves
together into words, nose to tail
in neon signs: *Liquor Store. Striptease.*
Once, serving scampi and garden
to madam, haddock and mushy
to sir, who had not swapped a word

or speculative confidence or thought
all night, Pearl placed the basket
of condiments – the vinegar, the salt,
the plump little pillows of tartare
and HP – at the edge of their table
so far beyond arm's reach that
to season their supper with acid,
mineral or herb, one of the pair
was going to have to, surely, crack.

Violette Pearl

What Pearl wears the first time
she goes to a night club is
a short grey shift sewn front
and back with silver spangles
and what she spots straight off
is not that the night indoors
is ageless and does not slip
like the night outside, nor
that the twelve-inch dance mix bass
makes ears of her bones,
but how the haze, the synthesis
of dry ice and Silk Cut smoke,
looks for all the world like
bluebells in a birch wood seen
from the far edge of a distant field.
At the bar, a spotlight hits the optics.
The beam shone through a litre
of gin splits into prisms of syrups
and spirits. Pearl orders cherry juice
and crème de violette. *I said*
she says to the barman *I said.*
This place. Is one. Where one.
Could start. To lay down habits.

The mirrorball is stuck all over
with square-inch glimpses of hooks
and drops and luxe and breaks
and fights and pills and skin.
What Pearl wears next time
is the same dress, plucked
of every shiny sequin,
their cotton threads
left nervous in the air.

Foaming Pearl

Then there was the year that Pearl –
like the celebrant of some celestial rite –
spent one white night in each of the town's
four hotels. The two star to the five star
list their ratings in a lowlight zodiac
on orange skies above the streets:
the constellating twinkle of The Iron,
The Chambermaid and The Minibar.
It's bedtime for the town when
all the guests have checked in for the night.
Pearl pours the whole small bottle
of foaming shower gel under a running tap,
dabbing lavender on the pulse-points
of her room. Then she plumps up
every order on the pillow menu, from
The Missing Marshmallow to The Body
in the Bed, and then an hour of flicking
through the channels on the air con: too hot
being shut-down, too cold and it's porn.

Hello Room Service, dials Pearl. *This is 452 –
I'm wondering if there's anything I can get
for you.* At three am, the tv offers decade-old
films or sitcom reruns. Pearl makes notes:
interpreter of other dreamers' dreams.

R.E.M. Pearl

The ushers, the bar-staff and the pyrotechnician
have all gone home, but up in the Green Room
Pearl discovers a lingering pair of magicians
who have missed the last call before lock-up
and are trick-stuck in competition. One's old-school
Variety, decked in a glitter tux and velvet dickie;
the other's street-sourced and tv-honed so wears
the same, though quote marks button up his cuffs.
Between them on the coffee table, two top hats.
The men are taking it in turns to thrust in their arms
right to their shoulders to grasp and then withdraw
a rabbit. Again and again they prestidigitate,

finagling the false bottoms and the laws of physics to dis- and re-appear their rabbits – the stoical buck and the impassive doe like all the rabbits you've ever seen before: the fur, the ears, buttonhole carnation scut, eyes like pink sweets, licked. Now you see them, now you don't. *Abracadabra!* cries one magician, hoarse. *Abracadabra!* cries the other, practically in tears. Pearl steps in. *O you wizards and illusionists! It's time to go, come on!* She picks up the pets and shepherds the magicians down the back stairs, through the stage door and out into the night, still cradling the animals' white weight. Even if they were to bite, their teeth are so sharp and so fine she'd barely feel the slightest bit of pain.

Tactical Pearl

The chicken-shaped timer pings
to let Pearl know her breakfast egg
has had five minutes and is cooked.
There should be cheers, she thinks.
There should be streamers and choruses
of *Auld Lang Syne* at every breakfast
when yesterdays, with their noisy campaigns
and tactical endeavours, cease.
Each Full English should bring a resolution –
the baked beans of *I will*, the bacon of *I won't*.
Another chance to get it right should spread
like marmalade on toast. Even a pastry,
the papers and two cigarettes are a kiss
on the cusp of something grown old
and something brand new. Pearl scoops
the egg from the boiling water and drops it
into its cup. The curve of the teaspoon
and the curve of the shell. Pearl
is a soldier; Pearl, the soft set sun.

ACKNOWLEDGEMENTS

'Helium Pearl' was commended in the Winchester Poetry Prize 2019

'Tartare Pearl' was first published in *Paper Trail* (Blown Rose, 2019).

'R.E.M Pearl' was inspired by the *Seinfeld* episode 'The Stakeout'.

I am very grateful to The Society of Authors and the Authors' Foundation and K Blundell Trust for their support.

Thank you to all the people whose poems I've read, and to the people who've read mine.

ABOUT THE POET

Julia Bird is a poet and poetry programmer. Her poetry collections *Hannah and the Monk* (2008) and *Twenty-four Seven Blossom* (2013) were published by Salt Publishing, and the illustrated pamphlet *Now You Can Look* (2017) by The Emma Press. With Mike Sims, she published the poetry and artist's book *Paper Trail* (Blown Rose, 2019) and *A Joy Forever: a walk out with John Keats* (Paekakariki Press, 2021).

She has worked for many poetry and literature organisations, and produces live literature shows through her company Jaybird Live Literature. More details at juliabird.wordpress.com

She currently works for The Poetry Society as Learning and Participation Manager, working on local and national events and participation activities for adults and young people. She grew up in Gloucestershire and lives in London.

ABOUT THE EMMA PRESS

The Emma Press is an independent publishing house based in the Jewellery Quarter, Birmingham, UK. It was founded in 2012 by Emma Dai'an Wright, and specialises in poetry, short fiction and children's books.

The Emma Press has been shortlisted for the Michael Marks Award for Poetry Pamphlet Publishers in 2014, 2015, 2016, 2018, and 2020, winning in 2016.

In 2020 The Emma Press received funding from Arts Council England's Elevate programme, developed to enhance the diversity of the arts and cultural sector by strengthening the resilience of diverse-led organisations.

Website: theemmapress.com
Facebook, Twitter and Instagram:
@TheEmmaPress